Exile Heart

poems by

Kim Shuck

Introduction by
Jenny L. Davis

Exile Heart

Collected Poems

Kim Shuck

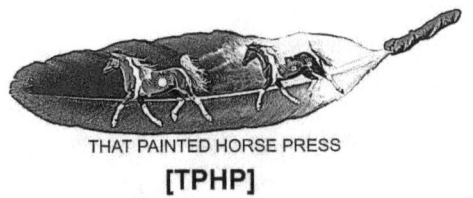

Harrah, Oklahoma
Calgary, Alberta
2021

Exile Heart

Collected Poems

Kim Shuck

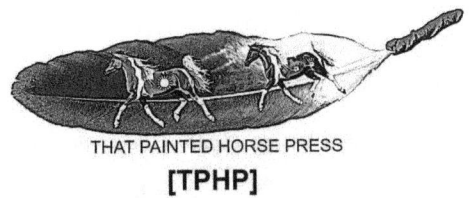

Harrah, Oklahoma
Calgary, Alberta
2021

Exile Heart

© 2021 by Kim Shuck

ISBN 978-1-928708-04-9

978-1-928708-04-9___

Except for fair use in reviews and/or scholarly considerations, no part of this book may be reproduced, performed, recorded, or otherwise transmitted without the written consent of the author and the permission of the publisher.

Cover Art: "Oklahoma" © 2020 Kim Shuck
Cover photograph © 2020 Douglas A Salin

Introduction © Jenny L. Davis
Author Photo © Douglas A Salin

Editor: Rain Prud'homme-Cranford
Editorial Assistant: Noémie Foley
Book Design: That Painted Horse Press RPC
Cover Design: Rain Prud'homme-Cranford

Native Writers' Circle of the Americas

[IPLC]
Indigenous Publishers
Literary Collective

That Painted Horse Press: A Borderless Indigenous/BIPOC
Press of the Americas
https://thatpaintedhorsepress.blogspot.com

Acknowledgements
Poems in this collection have been previously published in:
"Bloom," *Cape Cod Poetry Review*
"Because Poems Live Dangerous Lives," *Four Winds Magazine*
"Bridges and Crossroads," *Cutthroat Literary Journal*
"In the Walnut Grove," *West Trestle Review*
"Long Car Ride," *Sparkle and Blink Candlestick Point*
 "Water War," *Dialogo Caternary Speaking Truth To Power*

Books by Kim Shuck
Smuggling Cherokee, Greenfield Review Press 2005
Rabbit Stories, Poetic Matrix Press 2013
Clouds Running In, Taurean Horn Press 2014
Sidewalk NDN, FootHills Publishing 2014
Deer Trails: San Francisco Poet Laureate Series No. 7, City Lights Publishers 2019
Murdered Missing, FootHills Publishing 2019
Whose Water, Mammoth Publications 2020
Exile Heart, That Painted Horse Press 2021

Table of Tributaries

Dedication
Introduction..i

I. Creation Songs Near the Rivers

Memory and Water...2
Drink..3
Damp...4
We wanted Catfish and Wild Garlic.........................5
Arts of Patience..6
Tassling Corn..7
Highway..8
Poetry of Absence..9
If You are Heading Home..10
Grandma Knew Rivers...11
More River Song...12
Water Lullaby..13
Bridges and Crossroads...14
Frog..15
Bilingual..16
Walking Around Water...17

II. Sizzle in the Mother Fire

Headline..19
Belief...20
Bleed...21
Red Stone...22
Borrowed Wildfire...23
It Was Better..24
Blooming..25
Seasons Walking West..26
Among Other Works...27
Touch the Big Water...28
Medicine Show..29

Because Poems Live Dangerous Lives..30
Take a Dark Breath for Me...32
Another Weight..33
Borders Get in Through the Eyes..34
Duet with the American Indian Religious Freedom Act..............35
Teach Me..37
Listen...38
Sweat...39
New Moon of Gathering..40

III. We who Steal Ourselves back from the Songs

Thieves..42
Fair...43
Lichen...44
Ransom...45
In the Walnut Grove...46
From Muscogee..47
Just Now...48
Another Map..49
Dance and Dance..50
War...51
Cloud Bridges..52
Long Road Car..53
Near the Zinc Mines..54
Shhhh..55
Mirrors to Bury...56
Sunflowers...57
Parent and Child Cycle...58
Healing...61
Huckleberry..62

IV. Epilogue: Exile Heart

Exile Heart..64

Dedication

It would be impossible to thank all of the people who should be thanked. There will never be enough books, nor enough reader patience to read through it all. For complicated reasons thank you Evelyn Grey for being so disappointed that my work didn't rhyme. E.K. Keith and Mahealani Uchiyama, thank you for listening to my hysterical and self-centered quarantine monologues. Thanks to the seriously famous SW Native writer who was a complete jackass when we met for providing an example of bad behavior. With any luck I manage to avoid being that. Thank you all of the obvious people, there are reasons that writers thank their families: Ed and Morgan, for all of the reasons. Doug because I love that you painted the house purple. QR, Devorah, Avotcja, Susan, Nina, Ruth, Eric, Joyce, Carol Lee, Bill, Paul, Lourdes and Lauren, Peggy, Thea and Vince thank you for the various decades of private art/life tutoring. Finally, thank you if you made it this far.

Introduction
"From the Golden Gate Bridge to the Neosho River"

A reader unfamiliar with Kim Shuck's larger body of work will find the poems in *Exile Heart* that speak to the issues of water protection, Missing and Murdered Indigenous Women, wildfires, and environmental contamination reflect a perfectly timed collection. One that gives language to the some of the most pressing topics of the moment. But longstanding readers will know that *Exile Heart* is the eighth book and seventh poetry collection by Shuck, coming 15 years after her first book, *Smuggling Cherokee*. And this greater body of work shows that these are themes that Shuck has woven into her poetry for decades. This is, in part, prescient on the part of a poet who listens closely to water, crows, and the occasional trickster passing through, and, in part, a reflection of the depth to which Shuck's writing has always been grounded in the lived experience—the everyday, the ceremonial, and the everyday ceremonies.

Rather than writing for an audience looking for headdresses and teepees or staking claim to a competitive category of 'most authentic Native American,' Shuck's resonance, consistency, and authenticity instead comes through the rejection of colonial expectations of what it means to be Indian (or a poet) and the false dichotomies like urban/reservation; modern/traditional; or home/exile. It also comes from her willingness to address these topics directly poking gently at the absurdity of these expectations. During her inaugural speech as the 7th Poet Laureate of San Francisco, Shuck told the audience,

> I've been asked a lot of questions in the last couple of weeks since I was named poet laureate, and a lot of people have spoken of me as a Native American writer, which I am. But I can't help but remember the time my mother came to one of my art shows and looked at my bio, which has been edited

by the people at the gallery, and they had taken out the fact that I'm half Polish.

Similarly, in "Shhh" she tells us:
> I understand myself to be contested space
> Water and stone belong to the
> Translators of experience they will
> Vote and I will not be party to that

Importantly, complexity of family and history are the realm of "contested space" only when Native identity is assumed to be one-dimensional. This is where Shuck's craft in weaving multidimensionality out of words shows a deftness in form and position to simultaneously recognize and reject the expectation that women, Indigenous people, and artists are defined by patriarchal, colonial, and other dominant systems. While this work can be seen across many of her poems and collections, the poem "The Great Urban Indian Poem" in her 2014 collection, *Sidewalk NDN* is a wonderful example:

> (The Great Urban Indian Poem)
> Has already been written
> Most people missed it the
> Fancy dancer has finally finished his
> Urban regalia collected his last
> Windshield wiper blade for his Oklahoma/Oakland
> Back bustle complete with Harley gas cap rosette found
> Himself lining up next to a red-headed San Francisco girl
> Her shawl edge marked with graffiti from outside
> Of Eli's Mile High Club and John Lee played
> The two-step himself
>
> The great urban Indian poem is ongoing but
> Most people miss it because there will never be a release...

>   The tribes involved are conflicted because one of the
>   Poets has no CDIB card and the other is from an
>   Unrecognized band that had never been more
>   Than obscure and she refuses to wear
> >   The 'official' tribal dress because, well
> >   It's horrible and not even historically
> relevant...
>
>   The great urban Indian poem will be found
>   When you least expect it...

This reflexivity and humor in the face of stereotype is a thoroughfare across her work. Take this excerpt from the poem "Home Songs" from her first collection *Smuggling Cherokee* in 2005,

> 2.
> That dry cleaners is built
> On the most sacred spot
> In four counties.
>
> It was not intended as an act of irreverence.
> They didn't ask and we
> Were too embarrassed for them
> To say.
>
> Yea, sometimes I get angry.
> Most often when
> I can't find any dirty laundry
> So I can go pray.

   As an artist and activist that wears many hats, often quite literally, Shuck's poems speak to a wide variety of listeners, and her craft is honed against the fiercest of audiences—the elementary school children in San Francisco to whom she regularly teaches art. This intersection of art and community, activism and political engagement, is another mainstay of Shuck's poetry, and *Exile Heart* is no exception. The poem, "Duet with the American Indian Religious Freedom Act" is but one place where this comes to the fore. The topics of other poems, such as "Another Weight" and "Because Poems Live Dangerous Lives" will resonate with those familiar with Shuck's use of the poem-a-day action to draw attention to critical topics through a multi-day, daily invocation of structure, of language, of repetition of action and intent. In this realm, Shuck penned 55 poems about the meaning of the *Early Days* statue, a 124-year-old bronze statue celebrating colonial histories in California, in the run-up to the historic vote by the San Francisco's Board of Appeals that led to the statue's removal. A second poem-a-day action on the topic Missing and Murdered Indigenous Women, would become her fifth poetry collection, *Murdered, Missing* (Foothills Publishing, 2019). In this way, Shuck has never shied away from the responsibility and potential of poetry, nor from the traumatic topics too frequently at the center of her communities. Her poems look directly at the creative and destructive natures of fire, smoke, and blood. This is evidenced in "Blooming" where Shuck writes:

>touch on the
>Cones just so
>Just so and each one
>Blooms and
>Scatters

From the Golden Gate Bridge to the Neosho River, Shuck's poems are an invitation to see the places she knows and loves in new ways. The rhythms of San Francisco and Oklahoma form the call and response of Shuck's poetry where the spaces imagined as separate and different are, in fact, powerfully connected by rivers, sidewalks, deer trails, and roads. Her poems not only invoke the cadences of Southeastern stomp dances alongside the reverberations of the beat poets in City Lights Bookstore; she does it in such a way that we are left to wonder why we ever thought they wouldn't go together in the first place. It is no surprise then that *Exile Heart* is a traveling song for the roads between sites of home—home that draws on conversations with adolescent foxes, cats, catfish, cottonmouth snakes, crows, flickers, turtles, and locusts along the way. "Long Road Car" offers us a perfect example.

> Crossing and crossing the Truckee
> I unravel
> Am woven back San Francisco Bay to Neosho where my heart curls unfinished
> On the long road
> Some mountains are impatient some
> Creeks unhurried...
> In the car
> Cheek pressed to glass the Wasatch
> Hum stories of great blue heron
> Mumble water to salt
> Count time by birds
> In my grandmother's voice
> Some will think of this as metaphor
> Others recognize a feather when they see it...
> Like highway reflectors
> We can stay between the lines
> Can read history by this light
> Road spirits pulling us
> Towards the ache that might be healing

And finally, like so much of her poetry, this collection is an offering song to water, in the form of rivulets, rivers, cave-in ponds, plodding rain, arroyos, and creeks. It is, as one of my favorites of this collection, "Drink" ends, an invitation to a "Ceremony neither of us/ Had ever heard of" but which we will want to take part in again and again.

~Jenny L. Daivs
Urbana-Champaign
2020

I. Creation Songs Near the Rivers

Memory and Water

Weather has broken no
Rain for now and a painful
Clarity here in middle of the
Dark there are those who speak of the
End times and there always are
They just keep coming and yes there are
Premonitions and events that
Draw us over the doorsteps into
Some new thing something
Frightening the owl in the
Garden some kind of
Sign past avian hunger and this
Lack of news we have
Nothing for one another not
One open palm or
Kindness left just this
Tight breathing and a pretense that you'd
Think I'd be able to live with there are these
Agates burned on an alter to a thing that
Remembers burnt stone offerings that remembers
What this is about and good thing too
Because this is just something I was taught I'm
Happy that it is understood somewhere
If not by me

Drink

Water is often the
Cure in one form or other and
Something about the accidental but our
Drinking rain from each other's
Cupped hands tasted of intention of a
Plan that may not have belonged to either of us but
Something staged nevertheless it tasted of
Ginger and driving and slightly of
Citrus and even if it wasn't the cure
and even if we stand awkward in misstep
now it was well worth that moment
Of having my fingers
Lightly on your wrist
Laughing into a
Ceremony neither of us
Had ever heard of

Damp

Rattle the windows shake
Pelt and
Storm something
Twists my hair in the night not
Into knots but another thing
Writing in a language I can't
Read a message for your
Fingertips this
Headache also has needs here in the
City greyed by my
Age and this plodding rain and
Every new green thing in the
Garden every
Whimsical yearned for thing
Under a slick of April
Damp

We wanted Catfish and Wild Garlic

Together in silence a
Cottonmouth
Ripples across the
Cave-in pond who knows
What noun will hit on the
Bait a
Modified verb grabbed clean
From a nearby leaf and
Locusts sing our
Deep hopes back to us
Unrecognizable we wanted so
Little so little we
Wanted catfish and
Wild garlic wanted to
Feed these mad and
Beating creation songs near the
Rivers eye a
Place between worlds right down
Near the front of the stage

Arts of Patience

We've been collecting stairs for years
Stairs and the notion of stairs
Build with them like children do
Just like playing with blocks we will
Paint them with heart ideas with generational hope
May yet reach somewhere else we had in mind
We wanted so little in those days
Between bingo and
Collecting funerals
Houses subside and the
Screen door doesn't fit quite the
Hedge apples grow
Thorn and poison in the way that they have
We collect these things
Comb rivers and
Creeks the margins of change for things like
Glass bottles to exchange for bait
Catch other things we want too and all of my heroes
Were good at fileting fish
And we were in the living room
Gathering stairs in boxes and
Pressed flat in books and
Trying not to hide them
Trying not to feel guilty

Tassling Corn

Thunder storms
Lightening from cloud to cloud
Energy not grounding
Tight brick
Town seeds
Stand guard
Long tailed flickers
Perch and sway
Red brick warehouse
Guards
Herds
Looks west to rainclouds
Lifts her face to coming
Downpour

Highway

Route 66 was the river we all
Lived with knowing its
Habits and fauna the
Sacred diners and
Cafes on its
Shores and
Seasonal overflow over
Flow there is a
Mythology there that
Blurs between cultures no
Fred Harvey but it replaced the
Railroad next food
Second floor of the Big Teepee and sometimes a
Hawk not quite dead on
Blacktop the one that
Marked me with a
Clenching foot a
Reflex between
French toast
Scrambled eggs and cubed ham and
Tangy coffee when I still
Smoked cigarettes and
Grandpa had a
Bronze American
Leviathan the
Horehound drops
Jerky moccasins gas and incandescent constellations of
Towns at night telling their very own stories
Unknown to us so many
Ghosts along this river that we
Share these pinpricks of
Similarity these
Hauntings this
Long man such
Crime such
Home place

Poetry of Absence

Reflake edge of your
Elegant knife
I watched her
Writing blank verse on fogged window then
Pulling words like fine cordage from that
Cold
Rigid surface
Whatever will she weave?
Ravens have come to my windowsill
They tap
A code of beaks and wingspan
We chew nuts together and
Think collectively about rivers

If You are Heading Home

Don't pack heavy
There is a weight limit on those roads
Possible to stand on new bridges without fear the
Neosho is still singing songs not ones you learned there before
Then something like
A thought the same conversation
Mae's house is
Worse than gone and
There are things you couldn't bear to see that way
Some families are never from anywhere that keeps breathing
Not for long an
Illusion of solid underfoot
Of rock but those
Persistent dreams of falling
They will wake you if not on the lakeshore than there
By the bay

Grandma Knew Rivers

It's just a river but the name
Trips me up the
Bridges the mythology of
Route 66 all of the family
Stories running those shores and feeding
Pecans
Stories running to the
Missouri to the
Mississippi and to the
Gulf coast it's just a
River but my dad fished it we've seen
Buildings floating in the
Flood water seen whole trees yearning
Southward it's
Just a river but my grandma chose it and she
Knew rivers

More River Song

I grew up watching you
Dance the river
Give your precise self the one not
Touched by your misunderstood
Disease and the
Voice that you learned there and I my
Crayons and paper a
Storm pulling me to the river and those old
Mountain spirits and underground
Beings guardians of roots and
Uncut stone I
Grew watching you
Letting the river take everything from the
Center outward with that
Lessoned voice and your need for things that are
Poison to you and we can say that you
Rode out your own need for the invented dark
Became your own cure your
Disease and send your best self
Into the river I have
Stood bare to my thighs in that water and with my
Very own voice we sing together

Water Lullaby

Teach me the lullaby for baby rivulets
Burble croon of new creeks
We will dance
Open footed on pebble mud margin
Toes wide
Chill of infant water
Gasps
Cradled in muscle of arch
Grab of heel
Swing me in grip of mother water
Midstream song
Silver in my hair
Floating out in
Silver breathing water
Caressing silver flash fish
We will rock hips
Reach through ripples through palms
Dance the truth of water
Float me out into gulf with grandma water
Fanned thin
Diluted riverbed
Riverbank
River creature studies
Songs unspooling into every other song
Sing frogspawn
Dragonflies and
Cypress fingers driven deep and learning
Stand with me by the water
Sing mornings with me by the river
Paddle life with me on the bay
Let us protect each other
Here in this place and time
Let us protect each other

Bridges and Crossroads

WPA bridge over the Neosho I
Stood on it in full flood with my
Dad the water just
Kissing the underside of the boards the
River moans shivering up my legs it stood until a
Flood licked out the
Footings they
Replaced it but when I dream the Neosho
the old bridge is there

They took the zinc out until they hit the
Daylight of 3rd street you could
See the crack in the pavement
Looked like another pothole and there was
Sunlight in the mine
Sunlight just there with the
Dull ache of lead and the grim
Scowl of jack

Those cottonmouths know some songs too they
Know some fish songs and once crossing Tar Creek
Bridge a grandma snake got hit by a
Pickup and in her last breaths we
Drove up on her there like a burning
Library her songs falling away in curls
Taken by updrafts like smoke prayers near the water she
Looked me in the heart and whispered just the one secret

Frog

When the first four-legged frog cousin
Pulled herself out of water it wasn't rejection
Soft wet skin called her back again and again
Blood a
Contract with water a
Promise in the cells a
Rattle we pick up and hand on a
Moaning song that arches and
Clenches to
Bring our babies cradled in
Water a
Gift returned a
Rattle we pick up and
Hand over one
Generation to the next

Bilingual

Lightening become
Polygons we are water
Surrounded by water and the road
Floods at high tide I want to
See the flooded road be
Delayed by it watch
Minnows swimming there the
Redtail in a controlled crash into the
Eucalyptus and water and
Water and a language
Borrowed from water

Walking Around Water

Our bodies are creeks
that have slipped their banks
Walking around water
Going to water
Grandma pulled crawfish from her
foam white hair
laughed otter laughs
We find our level
Fall in breathy virga fall
Into floatingWe are creeks who dance with the
gator goddess we dance to the
drumming we are
floodwater we have slipped our banks
Grandpa knew fish
Dad knows dungeness and bullhead
We roll pebbles until they tell us what they know
We are overflow walking around water
Remember we are water
We sing water
We are young water
We stand with the water
Protect the water

II. Sizzle in the Mother Fire

Headline

Today the mother
Fire is silent
Navigational stones
Still the calendars the
Thunk of a boot on the
Deck of the Green Eyebrow and
Every interesting thing that
Happened the week the
Titanic sank a
Carefully carved bone
Hook is sunk
Past the barb and it has all of my
Focus

Belief

Today is a fighter with
Edges in cat ear tatters that poets
Read about safety of streets when he
Was young and the numbers
Don't
Don't agree but he believes it so he
Poems about it he is safer
Safer than ever but he
Remembers fondly the 1800s when he
Might have sold my head to the state some of us
Learn to curl up tight to build
Safety out of
Invisibility and some of us
can't breathe

Bleed

Impossible to write blood without
Weight of
Gender of
Potential feminism of
Let's face it
Melodrama and we say
Spill or draw or seep
Depending upon
Where and when and who and if I say that I am
      Bleeding I am bleeding

Like some creature or
Character from a lesson
Story which blood do we suppose I
Use for that offering? If I say that I am
      Bleeding blood I don't know

How to stop if I say that something was
Stuck here near my aortic or carotid or maybe
Femoral and I don't know any more than anyone if my
Yanking it free left something there that
Keeps me bleeding or maybe it's that
Internal calendar or maybe that
Time keeping is coming to an
End for me too and maybe I keep digging at the
Wound or maybe I'm just
Amazed again that I
Somehow keep making
so very much blood

Red Stone

What happens to the
Children of
Warrior families when they
Find themselves confronted with the
Fact of a spring full of
Apple blossoms and sleeping boys whose
Attendant cats drape like
Wisdom snakes and the
Wild rose sings something that might be
About England the
Early pinking houses on this hill whisper of
Light and controlling light and the
Angles it can reveal that might make you
Smile into this morning might
Make you want to be seen for yourself
Entire in some post
Invasion moment when we are
Not expected to forge
Prehistoric personalities or even
Excavate them from this
Quarry that can sometimes spit
Something as useful as flint and in such
Astounding colors too

Borrowed Wildfire

Smoke borrowed
Thunder
Mockingbirds
Screaming microwave alarms and
Next door the
Unregulated metronome of
Draining water in a
PVC pipe this silk the
Color of bruised berries this
Forest green the variegated
Grey of cloud cover still isn't a
Ceremonial dress and the
Skyshard off to the east so
Like something I have found on the
Beach a blue that clots in my
Throat the clear red of
Warning lights and
Supermarket signs today I
Want to sing a song of
Remembering my real name a
Song that doesn't jump at thunder of
Fire quenched in water or
Fire that
Knows not to take houses
Houses that
Must continue standing

It Was Better

Implication an
Innuendo I knew something about this but
Can't remember what that was like either
Morning of tracing regional maps that have
Been moved these star charts from
Somewhere specific and they can no
Longer tell us where that was this
Fingertip's route from Snake Mound to
Golden Gate Bridge to the ghost map of
Underground river there are seeds in this
Language not residue but
Bundled understanding that waits in
Speech and like telling cards or
Heat cracked shoulder blades or
Stirring water at dawn with
Practice it gets
All too easy to
Read

Blooming

Mother fire dragging herself through the
Dry licks and tastes she is the
Extreme cure singing
Shape shift songs singing
Change and heal
Toast and soup and the
Pines know their own
Ways to balance to
Call fog and harvest her
Thousand colors like
Fish scales they
Sizzle in the mother fire her
Muscles tight and
Feral the
Clench and release of her
Rummage through the rattlesnake grass and
Sumac and her touch on the
Cones just so
Just so and each one
Blooms and
Scatters

Seasons Walking West

Spring is another
Season of passing
Flowers dying to
Set fruit and that
Committed
Scorpio moon with
Everyone looking on the
Thick morning of
Ongoing heat singing into the
Past, to the east to the
People who take
Pieces of us with them and I
Shudder at what I'm
Missing this week at the things
I will miss

Among Other Works

Because people are not about hands and work but belief
Rodrigo decided what parts of my discovered body
Belonged to Spain it was early in a month of
Strawberries which are a true thing a
Thing that can be held in a hand but
Hands do not make a person
Because some people are not about hands and work but are owned
Imagination is a deep mine into the
Mountain of silver and both hands and silver can be
Hauled to the name of God and
Taken by boat to Spain and we know that
Silver can be a fact or an imaginary friend
Because belief is a hand that draws lines
We are a drawing that can only be seen from
Very close up or from very far away and
Only in a few languages
We did not break we were
Broken like lines in a poem, map or working hand
Because we believe that fingerprints and calluses can
Identify a person
Borders are dangerous are
Amputations that we carry like truth through stories and other stories
We carry them as though it is our work as though it were a
Strawberry we could hold in our hand

Touch the Big Water

They want to visit the
Pacific the guests that come here to touch
Big water no way to forget that it's sacred I
Point in the direction of Japan and we stare
Clear trembles of jellyfish desiccated
Sand dab shells and I promise there was the
Head of a cartoon Pocahontas tangled in
Bladder wrack sometimes I am the
Decapitated head and sometimes I am the
Water

They want to measure their
Authority against my 5'3"
Person to push against to
Collect my identity my ability to reason and
Walk in my own skin not
Camouflaged by
Position or borrowed feathers
Sometimes I'm Ersula Ore sometimes
I am Ersula Ore

They might want slide walls closed on the
Palace of Knossos and
Architecture leads us the water
Goddess and the monster and the
Trick mirrors and the sliding walls that
Only seem to close and the very short
Thread in slowly collapsing rooms and I am almost
Always face down with my cheek pressed to the
Hood of a car

Medicine Show

You are not a
Trickster god it's not
Something you find like cash
Someone left in the Goodwill
Coat or a pebble on the beach well ok
Maybe you can get it as a pebble on the
Beach but not by asking and there are things that
Evaporate if claimed and you and your
Generation claimed
Everything like some kind of skulk of
Adolescent foxes rubbing
Scent greed and
Territory and your survival doesn't make you right
Even if your tasteful
Robe of patchwork
Culture will sell for
Big bucks at
Christie's your
Sampler plate religion will set a
Trend your understanding has
Yet to touch anything as deep as a
Breath under the surface

Because Poems Live Dangerous Lives

Can't write the
Vanished poem the
Murdered poem she
Slips from under my pen off of
Pages in my notebook and
Every planned word needs
New plans

Last seen alive the
Murdered poem
Vanished poem was
Somewhere she shouldn't have been like
Walking or breathing or
Trying to see herself
Somewhere else

Vanished poem caught on
CCTV in
Vancouver or Winnipeg
Atlanta or Albuquerque
Leaving work heading
Home the murdered poem
Never got there

Because poems' lives are
Dangerous because
Every poem is a
Potential headline along
Highway 16 these poems
Run to Prince George or
Somewhere else

And if a poem
Steps off of a cliff while
Avoiding the police and if it can't
Fly then police cannot find that poem it

Takes family
Community and I
Still can't write her

Take a Dark Breath for Me

Tell me
How afraid are you of what we have become?
Step over your neighbor and quote to me
from books we've both read
Rain starts
A series of slow coughs
Another dark breath
Throw down and become the best
possible way of keeping score
Remote ego boost
Forgive yourself for what you like
Who you hate
Let's breathe dark together
A permanent scar
Late life ache
Rain continues

Another Weight

The Nina
Pinta and
Santa Maria have been
Carried overland for far too long
Every indigenous child handed a
Ballast stone at birth
Five adults
Mast on shoulder
Four young women untangling rigging and
Elders folding sun dried sails flaking with salt
Walking the southern wagon trails to the
Pacific like an unhealthy song
Singing everyone west for all time we have carried
Chris in our pockets our
Shoes are mudded with him and word of him our
Faces marked our hands
Muscle sore our
Voices frogged with
Songs of the lost the
Planks have been sent out into
California surf but they float back
Every
October they
Wash back up onshore

Borders Get in Through the Eyes

Some mornings we bring the
Border with us
Nothing is inexplicable you were a
Hostage to your
Gendered body
Respond faster
React faster the
Keys are complicated or illegal bound in with some
Confused moral scaffolding that still
Holds womanhood as
Judgement and we are judged by what we owe
Even to people we've never met never
Imagined you
Brought your borders with you and they are
Apt to expand without
Notice prone to
Mess slivers of border like the
Ice queen's shards might
Get in through the eyes and sing change
Vibrate change
People like us are
Unpredictable we are an
Inoculation we bring the
Borders along we
Bring them with us

Duet with the American Indian Religious Freedom Act

Another dancer got his feathers
Confiscated
Memory unrolls like an old photo
Flakey and brittle which
Dances we couldn't have and where we
Couldn't have them

Whereas the religious practices of the American Indian (as well as Native Alaskan and Hawaiian) are an integral part of their culture, tradition, and heritage, such practices forming the basis of Indian identity and value systems;

Up north the sacred places under water
Out east the sacred places under water
Shall we rename the months?
What month is it now?
I had hoped to raise my children not to be
Furtive not
Illegal, not vanished

Whereas the lack of a clear, comprehensive, and consistent Federal policy has often resulted in the abridgment of religious freedom for traditional American Indians;

Gazing into the night sky last week we wished on a
Falling law
Blew on dried
Law weed seeds and
Still waiting on
Results
Fell asleep to a story of keeping promises

Whereas such laws were designed for such worthwhile purposes as conservation and preservation of natural species and resources but were never intended to relate to Indian religious practices and, there, were passed without consideration of their effect on traditional American Indian religions;

Apache land sold to
Developers
Not years gone but
Now

Teach Me

Smoke by
Water and the soft taste of this
Week will you
Teach me to sleep with the
Light off again?
Smoke now and the
Song of packing
Bags the song of
Careful change
Lavender and
Peaches and this
Difficult and
Angled hope

Listen

Looking for an old story a
Story that has walked a
Few hillsides ravaged by
Wildfires a
Story that has been
Evacuated ahead of the flood
Carrying only a backpack full of
Photos and grandpa's
Gold watch I need a
Story that likes secondhand stores the
Sort where you can get a jar of
Mother of pearl buttons or a
Camel hair overcoat a story that
Collects scraps of lace and interesting
Hand tools I want an old story a
Story with experience of tragedy a story
Not ruined by it I want a hopeful story

Sweat

Fire will heat the stones and this is not my
Prayer but I love my cousins and it is theirs
We carefully press hands against the tender places
Barely healed
Injuries of you will not
You are not
We will move you
Forbid you
We will spin your eyes we will
Tear we will
Erase
Prayer smoke reknits cell to cell
Sings softly of
Being whole
What the hell Oakland?
Family and community
Throw pillow words
To cover violation
Fire and fire and the
Stubble of
Yearning growth is burned again
This fire heats the stones
The words that we
Lean into

New Moon of Gathering

Pulling bones around me in this new
Moon of gathering tucking in
Poppy seeds
Borage new
Wild strawberries holding close as
Much of this orange sky as I can and
Every ribbon and magnet and
Bead that I have is
Singing strange
Colors today singing quietly
Just now but
Who knows where this impulse is
Going?

III. We who Steal Ourselves back from Songs

Thieves

We who steal ourselves back
From songs and
Laws and habits that
Claim us and
Everything about us the
Long men the wide
Hipped and
Generous bays
Protective as any
Mother we who can
Still hear Lovejoy's press
Can hear it from under the water the
Supervisory singing wolves we
Who sing to other songs we
Steal ourselves back the
Kidnapped and hostaged the
Unransomed and unransomeable we learn
Songs to pick locks to
Absorb your laws and habits we are
Coming for ourselves we are on our
Way

Fair

Morning in a
Milk glass fog
Dime lands
Dead center sound of
Calliope shine off a
Painted horse's glass eye and
Smashed pennies
Increasingly baleful
Sky copper grey
Paint may be peeling on that
Tin sign but
Lights will always tug at me
Clang and ring and every such
Cliché but I fall for
Midway I
Give myself to it
Every coin operated
Fortune teller and
Toothpick county fair of it
Happy
With sand in my shoes and
Tongue red from
Candy floss

Lichen

Shushes a small grey green song
Damp
Sunless
Bay laurel rattles bright
Washed by recent and coming rain
Water is a song made of songs is the
Best of secrets and stories
Up north they're giving blood for water
Imagine every truth
Pressed against the welling of blood
I didn't raise children to be torn by panic to be
National sacrifice pass
Quiet prayers back and forth from
Pacific coast arroyos and
Creeks to
North country remind me
Remind me of the memory of this place I will
Tie every knot I ever learned to tell this story tie
Knots around the sharp and bitter points of cracked
Bone

Ransom

Somewhere there is a rock that
Fills your palm like a
Raven's breast
Waiting for a line or two to
Remind everyone what they
Already know about
Waiting for a heartbeat under fingertips about
Feathers black as Rome's ransom to
Huns and how much
Pepper would you pay how much is
That sense of wonder worth as
Chill pours in off of
Pacific and
Leaks through window where
Wood has pulled away from glass

In the Walnut Grove

That year the wind took the
Topsoil and the children the
Maps all changed and not
Everyone found a pair of
Magical shoes or good
Company I wonder if she paused
Every time she introduced herself if it
Was a question between her teeth as well the
Taproots that go somewhere
Unknown and we understand that
Every family has stories that are
Painted over there are always
Things hidden in the walls but when all you
Know is the blank wall and the
Hints and suggestions of what might be in there and you
Know, know that all of the expected
Family portraits are in ink only
Visible under a certain moon

From Muscogee

Air this morning smells like
Summer prayers
Dark v of flicker tail
Flicker tail
We whisper poems for navigation
make sure that we can find the way

I'm reminded that back in the city
Maya Angelou used to drive a bus
Because poems are a better map
Draw lines wide enough for a
Foot or a
Bus tire

Just Now

All yesterday the rain and you
Know that we yearn for it
Hiccup and dig of a stomp dance but we
Needed today I wouldn't like to guess how you do it
But it's not wet now
Crazy light to east under
Irritated clouds
Blue hills across bay and all of these
Gridded and neutral
Buildings downtown they are following
Wounded rhinos in Mozambique just
Near the border some
Notion of potency that
Days long suffering speaking to
Some form of power perhaps but this
Weather these well
Danced pavements the morning
Raven with his memory of roasted
Almonds in my breast pocket or
Failing that a willingness to flip rocks oh
Love I just want to sit here with my head against your
Knee just want to sing along to a
Politics I trust even if I don't
Always understand

Another Map

Catch the trees
Ringing first thing
Chiming about
Anything but their
Deepest held
Secrets something about
Rum and
Raspberries and
Star charts that show
Movement as well as relative
Positions I can't hold my
Breath as long as that bay laurel still
One morning I caught their
Ringing in an old
Silver locket and am
Saving the sound for a
Desperate occasion

Dance and Dance

Today I danced in
Congo square in
Communion with drums and
Ankle bells still
Cradled in some
Parallel and
Resonant sidestep my
Leaf-like fingers shifting in
Other air in
Yearning with other people
Finding water's level

War

And in the water war we will
Paint signs of bravery and
Protection onto the
Salmon the
Trout and wade into the
Streams with them and they will
Paint us back in the
War of clear water we will
Insist that water be local and when it
Can't be local we will weigh the benefit to the
Real costs of lawns in the
Desert or apricots and almonds we will
Seek to understand other people's
Prayers and what gets flooded by
Dams or drained by canals and
Will consult the birds about the
Wetlands and they might paint us too and the
Consulting board will offer seats to pines and
Sunflowers who defended the people the
Last time and the wolves and beavers who change the
Streams will also be heard and we
Cannot lose cannot
Lose

Cloud Bridges

Touch and
Break
Come together
Clutch then release their own
Symbolic selves
We storm
Flash
Sing air and sky
Moment poems and
Nothing lasts longer than this
We storm
Listen

Long Road Car

Crossing and crossing the Truckee
I unravel
Am woven back San Francisco Bay to Neosho where
my heart curls unfinished
On the long road
Some mountains are impatient some
Creeks unhurried
Stripers arranging
Songs coded in gill and
Fin

Fan meltwater to prayer
Something they can dance to
In the car
Cheek pressed to glass the Wasatch
Hum stories of great blue heron
Mumble water to salt
Count time by birds
In my grandmother's voice
Some will think of this as metaphor
Others recognize a feather when they see it

At night
With all of the bird thoughts
Caught in my hair
Like highway reflectors
We can stay between the lines
Can read history by this light
Road spirits pulling us
Towards the ache that might be healing

Near the Zinc Mines

I can see the signs of jack in your eyes and you
Caught the hint of flicker tail feathers in my hair
We make each other visible
Creekwater
Gravy in a cast iron skillet the
Coming storm rolls east
We make each other visible
On holy days and at any other time
Red clay dust at our ankles
Creekwater
Cress
Hardshells
Terrapin basking
We make each other visible
Hum of locust ritual

Shhhh

I understand myself to be contested space
Water and stone belong to the
Translators of experience they will
Vote and I will not be party to that
I understand myself to be a
Resource
Water and stone and my
Translated bones will not sift and
Dream but where the voting says they will
                              Shhhhhh
Songs belong to the stealers of songs they
Comb my disordered thoughts and
Any song that comes from them will also belong to the
Thieves who can reclaim them and my other thoughts at will
This place is myself and I
Understand it as family and breath
Translated and catalogued
Taken and arranged in the latest style
We have not gone
                              we are not gone

Mirrors to Bury

We still have
Mirrors to bury
Walking north I
Know this water we
Should be catching up on old news
Don't worry I
Know my way home from here
"Repentance is a matter of the
Heart" and not the business of the courts but
Conscience is
I know this water the
Pebble and
Sigh of it and
Words are
Stolen from where they sit
Cooling
One by one
"It was said"
The water knows you
We are walking
North with the poems I am
Burying mirror after
Mirror for
Navigation for
Poet after poet

Sunflowers

Arrive at the front door they
Pick through beads they
Stare through them
Whisper poems to pines
One word at a time
Because these days are short
Every seed watches and
Who knows what they are thinking?
Generational affiliation I find dried seeds in toes of my shoes
Singing of dancing of
Medicine I find dried seeds
Every day closer to the creek
It isn't patience but hunger

Parent and Child Cycle

1.

When the first pain hit
I went up on my toes
Birth dances you
And all of the people that will breathe at you
Speaking for my self
They were of no help
My son and I
We did that dance together
Became two people
Another kind of storytelling

2.

We took the stereotypes in our hands and
Tore them up
The worlds we have created between us
Parent and child
Person and person
You
Curled there and whispered stories of healing into my fever dreams
We have adventured

3.

Cleaning grandpa's desk we found the
Mary of Czestochowa
Her black skin rendered in silver metal
Isis by any other name
Still brought her lover back from the dead
And claimed a son from him
Isis of sky and wisdom
Wrapped in blue
As I have been
Just feeling the heartbeat

The damp skin
The wonder of a new person

4.

We carefully mark the places where the world changes
Pack our borders our toothbrushes
Walking shoes
Rewritten in every watershed every
Story shed
Children of corn
Walking north
The sons of corn
Performed the magic as they were taught
And the people were fed
We are dusted with pollen we are
Walking north

5.

The child shows me the mark of the scorpion on his leg
I show him the mark of the spider on mine
We have walked dangerous miles
He and I
Separate parts of the same story
The gods took a handful of corn flour
Some blood and
We are born
Danced
Went up on our toes
You may have been born differently
But this is our story

6.

Children in cages
Dis-prayer
And genetic memory offers a panic
Stolen children

The sacred geometry
Shattered
We carry our borders
We who are blood and corn
We reach across rivers
We call to our cousins
We burn the copal

7.

This part of the poem isn't written yet
We have to write it together.

Healing

Goddess disassembled and reworked the
Ordered angles a
Scientific method that imagines
Control of one
Variable at a time and the
Monarchs fall a
Complicated leaf cover speaking of a new kind of season
Goddess endangered the
Black snake
Scales whispering of gold of
Fruit as if we were all
Walled gardens as if the
Spirals of intention the part and
Spill can tear themselves from
Entropy and unbreak
Unsteal
Can unmix in a dance that we have
Passed like a secret of rattle and
Shell and dance that we are called to
Again
Now in trust
Dance with me

Huckleberry

This time of year can be used for treating pain
Everything is a cure for something
The cause of something
I don't know if these prayers are holy
Words
Created sounds
Vibrations
We put them into the air
Into our walls
Take them back through our skin

IV. Epilogue: Exile Heart

Exile Heart

How many generations will the
Exile's heart be passed
Gene to gene the story of
Berries by the river and the near
Words muttered by a wind through the
Rocks on a hill even when the
Hand that remembered a rock that fit a
Child's palm in
Just this way a
Rock she wished on or the
Climbing tree and these
New holidays these new ways don't
Hold water when the wind is from the north and that
Precise rain starts
Falling

Kim Shuck — photo credit: ©2020 Douglas A. Salin

Kim Shuck: Kim Shuck was born in San Francisco, California, and is a member of the Cherokee Nation of Oklahoma on her father's side and also of Polish descent through her mother. She received a BA in Art and an MFA in Textiles from San Francisco State University. Shuck is the author of *Deer Trails* (City Lights Books, 2019), *Clouds Running In* (Taurean Horn Press, 2014), *Rabbit Stories* (Poetic Matrix Press, 2013), and *Smuggling Cherokee* (Greenfield Review Press, 2005), as well as of the chapbook collection *Sidewalk NDN* (FootHills Press, 2018). In 2019, Shuck was named an **Academy of American Poets Laureate Fellow**. She most recently served as the Poet Laureate of San Francisco, California.

Jenny L. Davis PhD: is a citizen of the Chickasaw Nation and an Associate Professor of Anthropology and American Indian Studies at the University of Illinois, Urbana-Champaign where she is the director of the American Indian Studies Program. She is the 2019-2023 Chancellor's Fellow of Indigenous Research & Ethics. Her research focuses on contemporary Indigenous language revitalization; Indigenous gender and sexuality; and collaborative methods, ethics, and repatriation in Indigenous research. Her  research has been published in the *Annual Review of Anthropology, American Anthropologist, Gender & Language, Language in Society,* and the *Review of International American Studies (RIAS),* among others. She is the recipient of two book prizes: the 2019 Beatrice Medicine Award from the Association for the Study of American Indian Literatures for *Talking Indian: Identity and Language Revitalization in the Chickasaw Renaissance* (University of Arizona Press, 2018) and the 2014 Ruth Benedict Book Prize from the Association for Queer Anthropology and the American Anthropological Association for her co-edited volume *Queer Excursions: Retheorizing Binaries in Language, Gender, and Sexuality* (Oxford University Press, 2014). Her creative work has most recently been published and *Transmotion; Anomaly; Santa Ana River Review; Broadsided; North Dakota Quarterly; Yellow Medicine Review; As/Us; Raven Chronicles;* and *Resist Much/Obey Little: Inaugural Poems to the Resistance* and exhibited at the Ziibiwing Center of Anishinabe Culture & Lifeways and the Minnesota Center for Book Arts.

A young child, just three years old when her mother died; A young woman, determined to live a life of faith & strength; An older woman expressing her wisdom, laughter, regret, love in a unique way.

All three of these women are Massell Smith. Her story begins in the 1940's. Through poetry and prose, Massell overcomes life's obstacles – she falls and gets up, dusts herself off, and starts over again. Tomorrow will always be a better way. The sun will shine. It's not easy, but her faith grows stronger each and every day. She has seen some of her dreams unrealized and others come to life in a fantastic way. When something is taken, something is given.

Through her words, Massell hopes to encourage others not to give up and to live life without regret and filled with love.

Massell Smith was born in the West Indies, in Jamaica, in 1944. Right after High School, she got a job for six months, in the ministry of education. After that, she was in charge of a boutique mainly for tourism. She had a full life.

Following surgery to remove a brain tumor in 1999, she was left with a communication disorder called aphasia. Client of the Aphasia Institute was a prior to be her stroke in 1999. With her own determination and the support of the renowned Aphasia Institute, the former medical laboratory technician now participates in conversation groups, paints, sings, is the president of a local Toastmasters club, and writes poetry and prose in her unique voice.